Jane Shirreff, Mary Anne Shirreff

Collection of sheet music from the late 18th and early 19th Centuries

Jane Shirreff, Mary Anne Shirreff

Collection of sheet music from the late 18th and early 19th Centuries

ISBN/EAN: 9783741116810

Manufactured in Europe, USA, Canada, Australia, Japa

Cover: Foto ©Angelika Wolter / pixelio.de

Manufactured and distributed by brebook publishing software (www.brebook.com)

Jane Shirreff, Mary Anne Shirreff

Collection of sheet music from the late 18th and early 19th Centuries

22

Steibelt – Op. 33.

Steibelt–Op: 33.

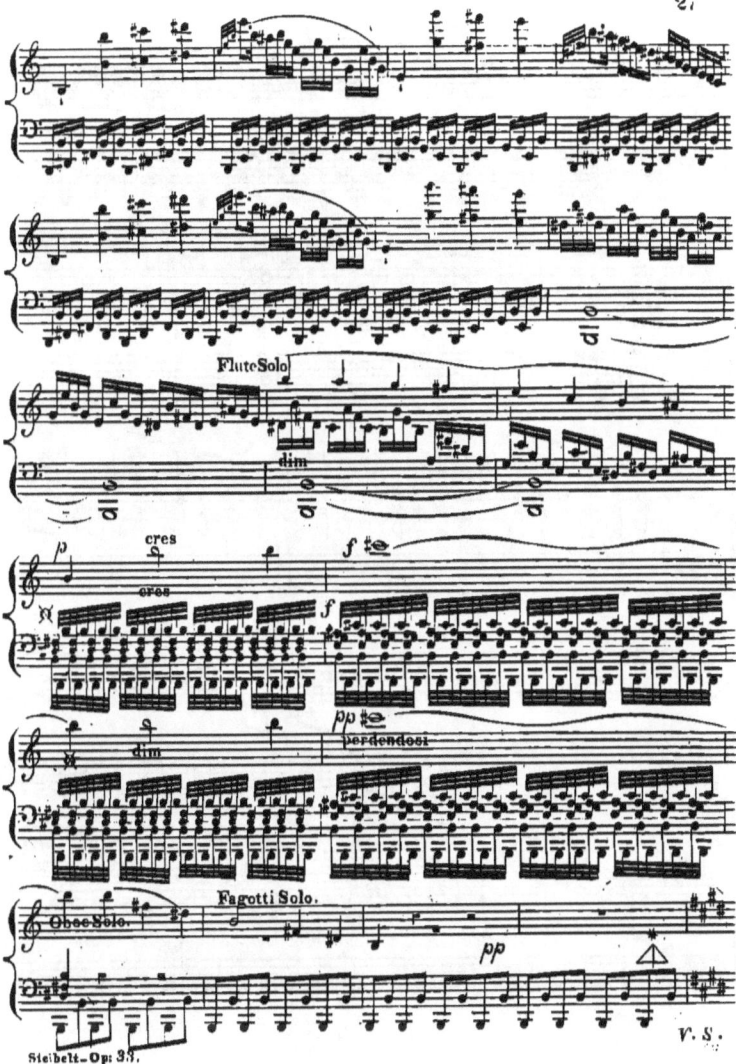

Steibelt – Op: 33.

THEMA
M Mozart ..
Nº 1.

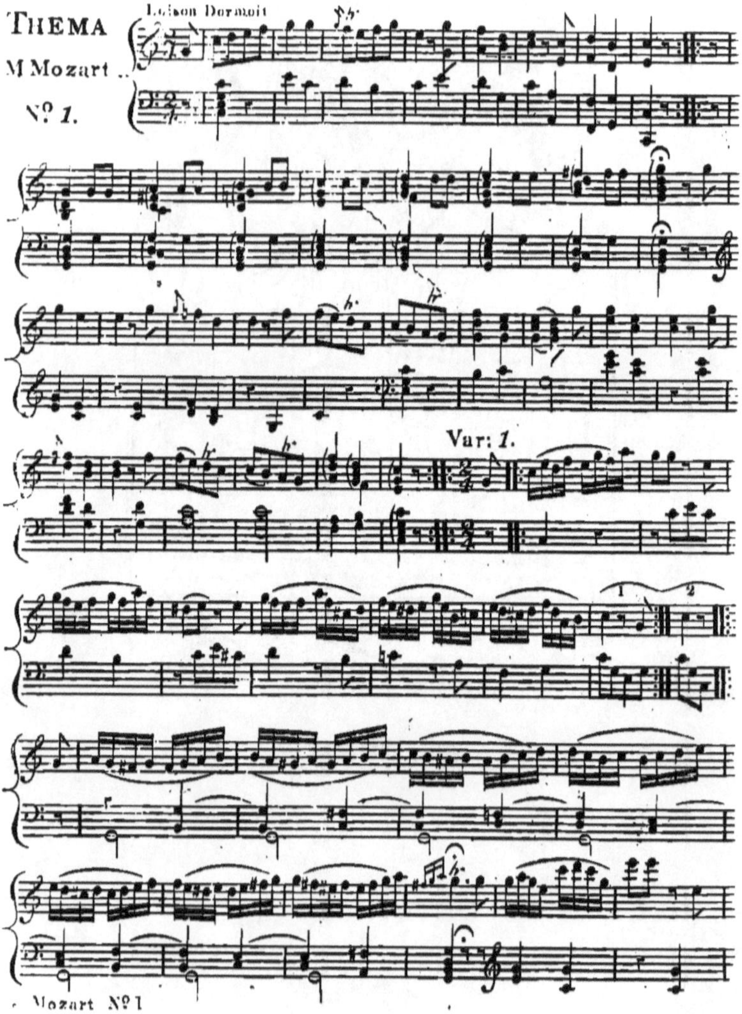

Mozart No 1

Var:7.

Mozart N° 1.

Mozart No 1

Selections From Mozart's Celebrated Operas,
NOW PUBLISHING.
Arranged by J. MAZZINGHI.

Le Nozze di Figaro.
Il Don Giovanni.
La Clemenza di Tito.
Cosi fan Tutte.
Il Flauto Magico, or Zauberflote.

} ARRANGED in Numbers Price 6/ each, for the PIANO FORTE, HARP, FLUTE & VIOLONCELLO.

Also the same Operas, with the same Accompaniments in One Book.

Le Nozze di Figaro.
Il Don Giovanni.
La Clemenza di Tito.
Cosi fan Tutte.
Il Flauto Magico, or Zauberflote.

} ARRANGED in Numbers Price 4/ each, for the PIANO FORTE, FLUTE & VIOLONCELLO.

Also the same Operas, with the same Accompaniments in One Book.

SINGLE OVERTURES.

Le Nozze di Figaro.
Il Don Giovanni.
La Clemenza di Tito.
Cosi fan Tutte.
Il Flauto Magico, or Zauberflote.

} ARRANGED for the PIANO FORTE, FLUTE, AND VIOLONCELLO.

SELECTIONS from IL DON GIOVANNI, arranged for Two Performers on the PIANO FORTE, either in Numbers or One Book.

Batti, Batti, O bel Masetto, with Variations for the PIANO FORTE, HARP, FLUTE, AND VIOLONCELLO.

} Also ARRANGED for the PIANO FORTE, FLUTE, AND VIOLONCELLO.

LONDON, Printed by Goulding, D'Almaine, Potter & C.º 20, Soho Squ.e & to be had at 7, Westmorland S.t DUBLIN.

PRIMO

Ov: La Clemenza D.

SECONDO

Ov: La Clemenza D.

A Sonata for the Grand or Small Piano Forte with Additional keys, Composed & Dedicated to Mrs Chinnery by J. L. Dufseck.

Op. 24. Pr. 2/6.

London, Printed by Goulding & Comp.^y 20, Soho Sq. Sold also at 7, Westmorland Street, Dublin. Where may be had all the above Authors Works.

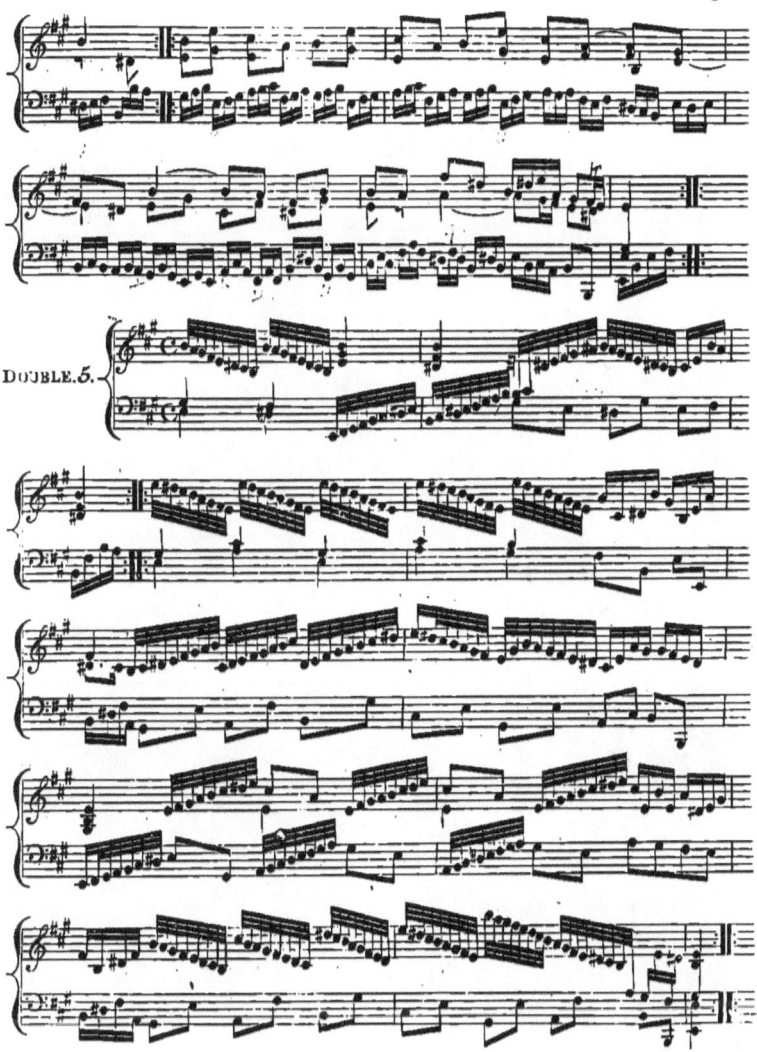

Horn's Rondo

Ma donne amore
Che importa se fallace
Piacer verace
E quel che solo ci da. Fine.
Guerra diletta
Val piu che oziosa pace

Laccio che aletta
Val piu che liberta
. Ma un. dolce si .
Compensa ogni dolore.

. Da Capo. Ah donne amore &c.

An Italian Ariette,
With an Accompaniment for the Piano Forte.
Composed by Sig.r Majer.

Ent. at Sta. Hall.

Price 1/-

London, Printed by Goulding, D'Almaine, Potter & Co.
20, Soho Square & to be had at 7, Westmorland Str, Dublin.

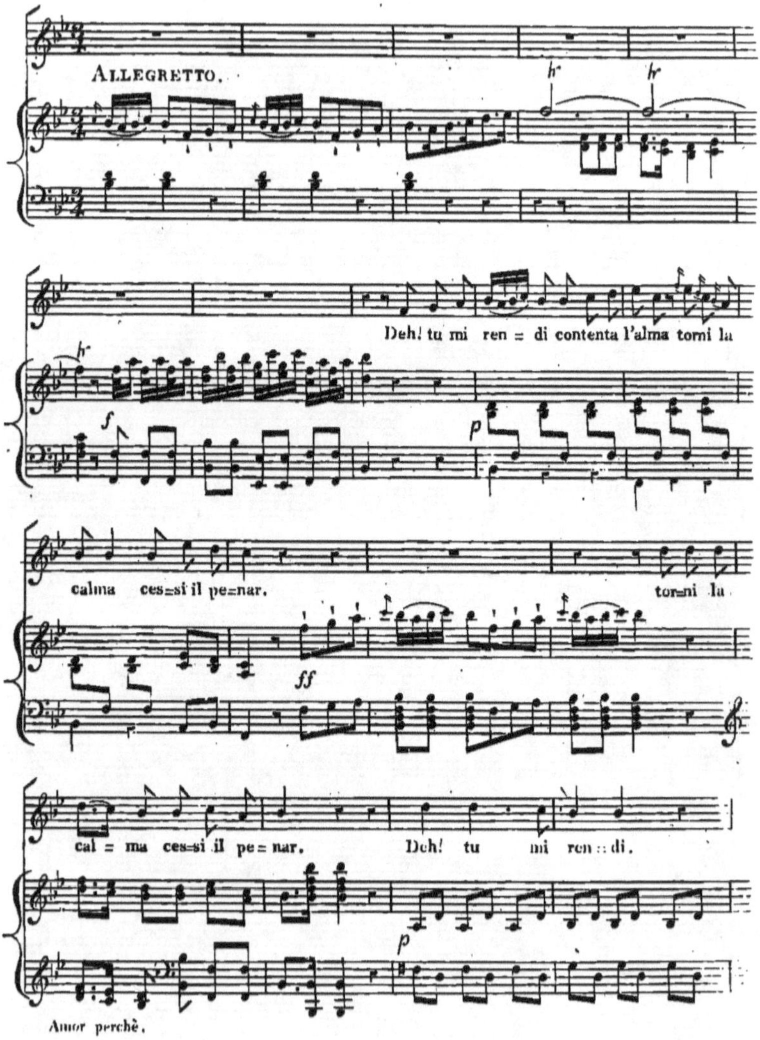
Allegretto.
Deh! tu mi ren = di contenta l'alma torni la
calma ces=si il pe=nar.
tor=ni la
cal = ma ces=si il pe = nar.
Deh! tu mi ren :: di.

Amor perchè.

Tu che Accendi

Cavatina,
Sung by
Mrs ASHE,
With Enthusiastic Applause
at the
Bath Concerts,
COMPOSED
With an Accompaniment for the
PIANO FORTE,
BY
Signor Rossini

Price 2/6

London, Published by Goulding, D'Almaine, Potter & Co.
20 Soho Square, & to be had at 7, Westmoreland Street, Dublin.

Tu che accendi

Fra tante angoscie e palpiti
CAVATINA,
introduced & sung by Signor Torri
in the Opera of
LA CENERENTOLA,
Composed by
SIGNOR CARAFA,
arranged & dedicated to
Lady Julia Gore
BY
C. M. SOLA.

Price 2:6.^d

LONDON,
Printed & Sold by Messrs Birchall & Co 133, New Bond Street.

Fra tante Angoscie.

Fra tante Angoscie.

Fra tante Angoscie.

Fra tante Angoscie.

Fra tante Angoscie.

Fra tante Angoscie

Fra tante Angoscie.

Per lui che adoro

Per lui che adoro

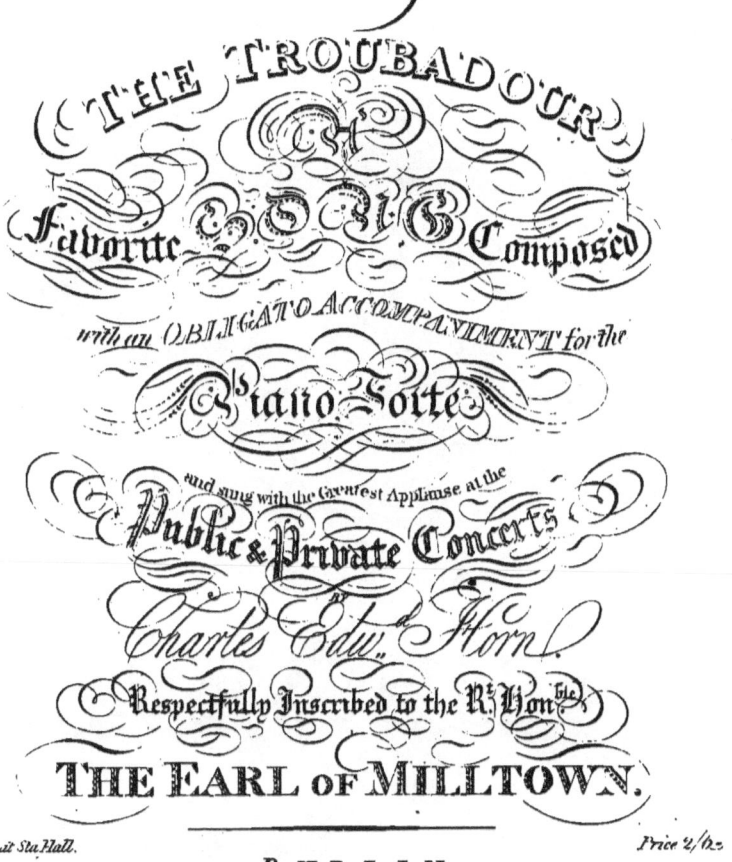

Comedy of Errors.

Comedy of Errors.

Henri Quatre

Henri Quatre

Henri Quatre

Henri Quatre

"Now place your hand in mine dear"

THE
Celebrated Duetto

sung by
Miss Stephens & Mr Duruset

In the Opera called

DON JUAN,

OR

The Libertine

at the
Theatre Royal, Covent Garden.

Composed by Mozart.

Adapted to the English Stage,
AND
Arranged from the Score
BY

HENRY R. BISHOP

Composer & Director of the Music to the Theatre Royal Covent Garden

7s^d —

LONDON.

Published by Goulding, D'Almaine, Potter & Co 20 Soho Sq^r & sold at 7 Westmoreland St. Dublin.

DUETTO

Sung by Miss Stephens & Mr Jarvis(?)

ANDANTE

Now place your hand in mine, dear, And gently whisper, yes, Each scruple now resign, dear, And poor Masetto bless! I would, but yet I would not; This wav'ring fickle heart, It beats for what it should not, Yet from thee cannot part, Yet from thee cannot part.

Libertine

LOVE the SIRE of pleasing fears,
SORROW Smiling thro' her tears;
And mindful of the past employ,
Mem'ry bosom spring of joy.

Fly to the Desert,

A Ballad,

from "LALLA ROOKH,"

Written by *Thomas Moore Esq.*

Composed by

G. KIALLMARK.

Ent. at Sta. Hall.   Price 2/-

LONDON,
Published by J. Power, 34, Strand.

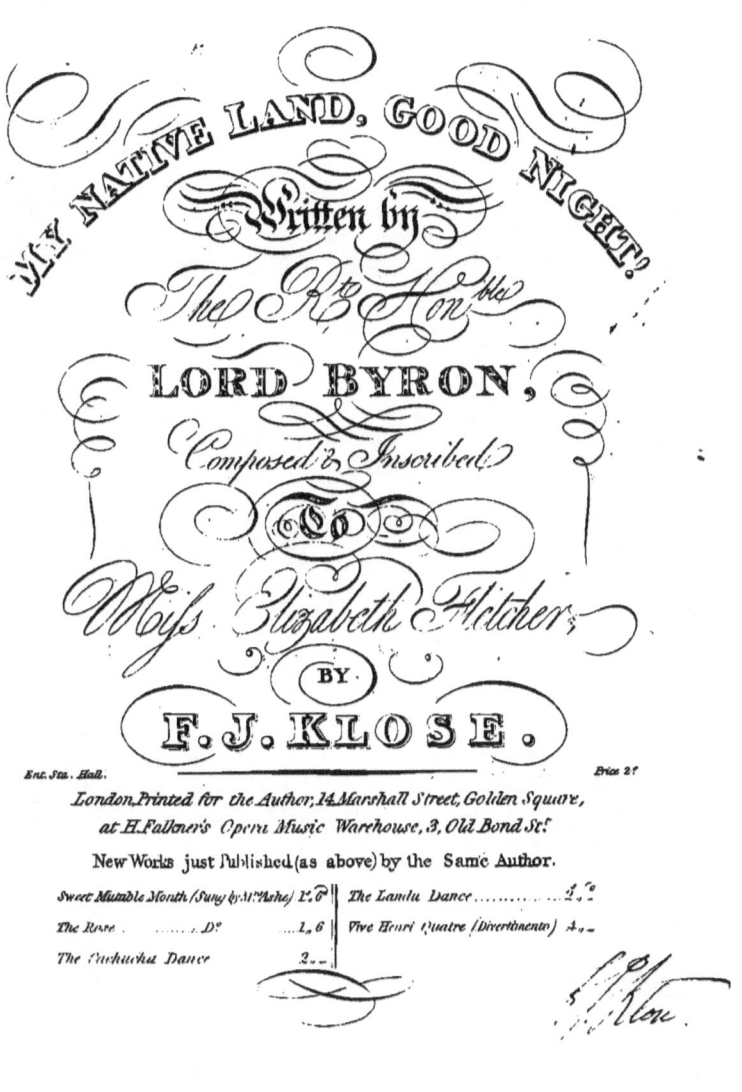

My Native Land, Good Night.

This Rose to calm my Brother's cares

The words taken from the Celebrated Poem of the

BRIDE OF ABYDOS,

The Music composed & arranged for the

Piano Forte,

by

I. Nathan,

And most respectfully dedicated to

LORD BYRON.

Published at Falkners, Opera Music Warehouse, N.º 3, Old Bond St.

"Thou art not false, but thou art fickle,"

The Poetry by
The Right Honble
LORD BYRON,
The Music Composed
With an accomp.^t for the
Piano Forte,
By
I. NATHAN.

Ent. at Stat. Hall.   Price 2/6.

Sold at White's Music and Musical Instrument Warehouse,
N.o 5 George Street, Bath.
Where may be had the Hebrew Melodies & the Whole of this Author's Works.

4

MY LIFE, I LOVE YOU.

In submitting this Music to the candid decision of the Public, it may be proper to observe, that every stanza of the Song, which is selected from the Poems subjoined to Lord Byron's "Childe Harold's Pilgrimage", concludes with the words Ζωή μȣ, σάς ἀγαπώ, a Romaic expression of tenderness, for which I have taken the liberty of substituting his Lordship's translation "My Life, I love you." In the third stanza, the vow "By all the token flowers &c." means those flowers which a lover sends to his mistress as a mark of his affection; for, as ladies in the East are not taught to write, lest they should scribble assignations, the sentiments of the parties are conveyed by flowers, cinders, pebbles &c. which have different significations. A bunch of flowers tied with hair, implies "Take me and fly."

I. Nathan.

Maid of Athens, 'ere we part, Give, oh, give me back my heart!

2

Remember me when eer you sigh
Be it at midnight's silent hour
Remember me and think that I
Return thy sigh and feel it's pow'r
When e'er you think on those away
Or when you bend the pious knee
Or when your thoughts to pleasures stray
O then dear maid remember me.

GERMAN FLUTE.

CATALOGUE OF BOOKS

Written, Published and Sold by G. WALKER 106 Great Portland Street.

THE VAGABOND. Dedicated to the Bishop of Landaff. — 2 Vols: Price 8^s: 0^d.

THE THREE SPANIARDS. — — — a Romance — — — 3 Vols: Price 12:6

DON RAPHAEL. — — — — — — — a Romance — — — 3 Vols: Price 13:6

POEMS, on various Subjects, with an elegant plate printed on fine paper — — — — — — —) — — boards — — 4:6

TWO GIRLS OF EIGHTEEN — 2 Vol. — by an old Man — — — — 8:0

MUSIC just Published, the words by G. Walker.

Remember me, from Don Raphael, Composed by Whitaker — — — — — — 1.
The Pilgrim Boy. — — D^o — — — — — — — D^o — — — — — — 1.
Blooming Virgins. — — D^o — — — — — — — D^o — — — — — — 1.
Go gentle Sigh, from the Three Spaniards. — — — — D^o — — — — — — 1.
Ye Maidens fair. — — — D^o — — — — — — D^o — — — — — — 1.
Art thou awake, — Serenade — — D^o — — — — D^o — — — — — — 1.
The Valentine. by Whitaker — — — — elegantly ornamented — — — — — 1:6
Six English Ballads, Op: 3. Composed by W. F. Crouch.
Viz:
How pleasing when the sun descends. —)
Be true to me my Anna cried. — — — |
Can I forget. — — — — — — — — — |
Why waves the banner. — — — — — — } — — — — — — — 7:6
It was a Knight in armour green. — — |
Are these then the scenes. — — — —)

—2—

Oh! 'tis sad when joys are blighted
In the beauty of their bloom,
When the form that once delighted
Withers in the silent Tomb!
Tears may tell a Nation's feeling
In the fullness of their flow
But the grief that shuns revealing
Who can paint — Affection's woe!

Weep! oh weep

—3—

Lovely as the Star of Morning
In retiring splendour drest,
Rich in all the mind's adorning
Peace and Love her pillow blest:
Daughter of our Land! the Dearest!
Albion's Hope and Brunswick's fame
Fairest Flow'r! amid the fairest!
Wept and hallow'd be Thy name!

Engraved by R! Taylor.

MOURN ENGLAND MOURN.

AN ELEGY

Written & Composed

ON THE LAMENTABLE DEMISE

of

Her Royal Highness

THE

Princess Charlotte of Wales.

BY

JOHN PARRY.

Ent.d at Sta Hall, ——————————— Price 1/6.

Her Royal Highness the Princess Charlotte of Wales, Consort of the Prince Saxe Coburg, died at Claremont, about half past 2 o Clock, on Thursday morning Nov.r 6. 1817. Aged 21 Years & 10 months, Having given Birth to a still born Son, about 9 o Clock the preceding Evening.——

LONDON.
Printed & Sold at Bland & Weller's Music Warehouse 23. Oxford Street.

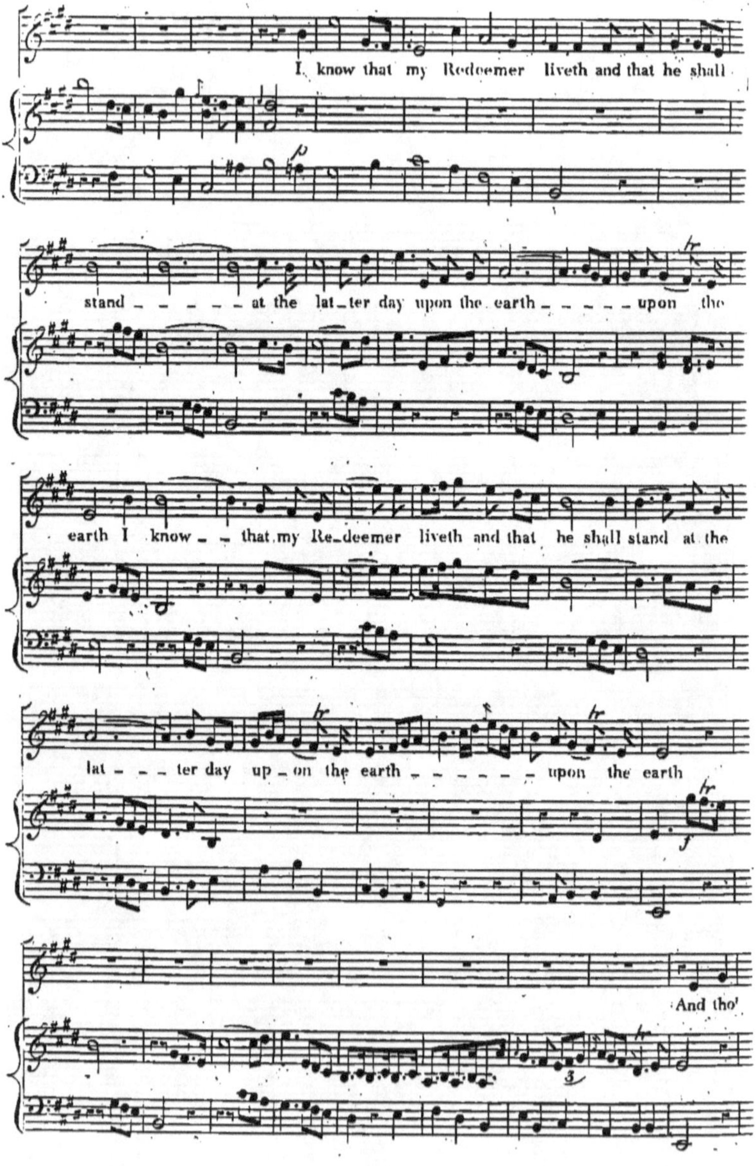
I know that my Redeemer liveth and that he shall
stand - - - - - - at the lat_ter day upon the earth - - - - - upon the
earth I know - - that my Re_deemer liveth and that he shall stand at the
lat - - - ter day up_on the earth - - - - - - upon the earth
And tho'

ANGELS EVER BRIGHT AND FAIR.
BY HANDEL.

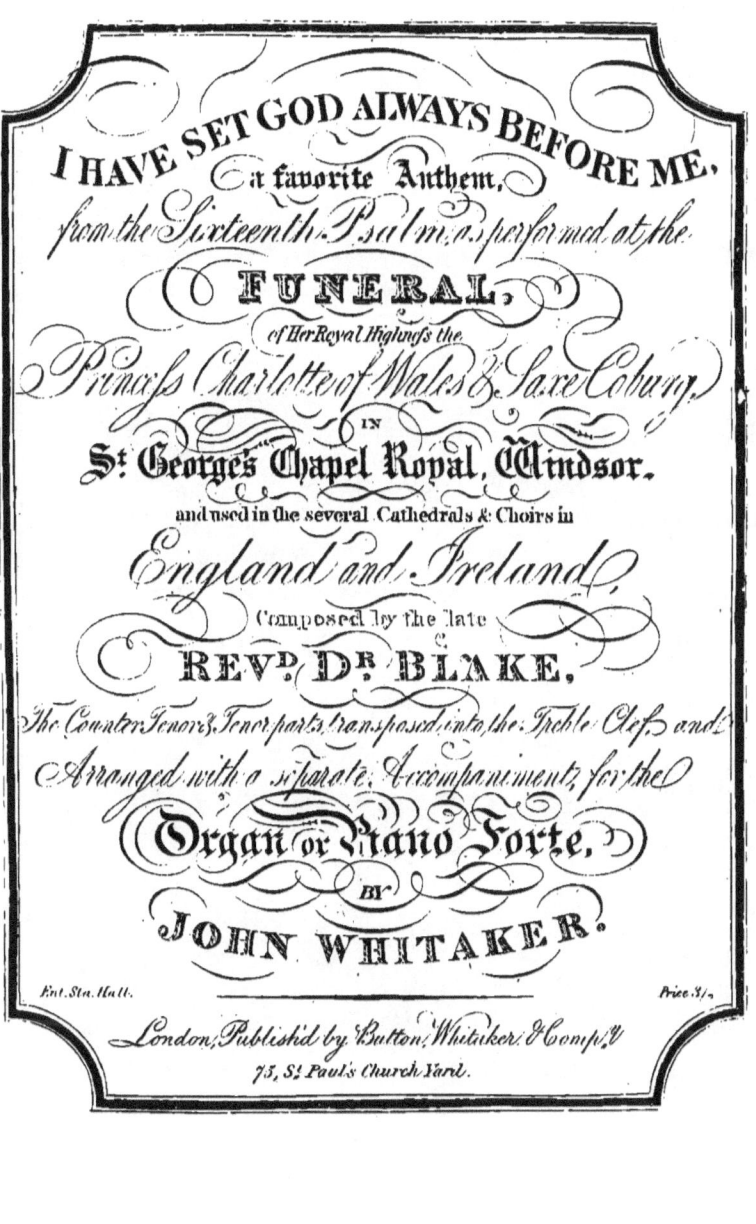

POLISH WALTZ.

N° 7.
VIVACE

FRENCH WALTZ.

NEAPOLITAN WALTZ.

Nº 9.

SPANISH WALTZ

Nº 11.

www.ingramcontent.com/pod-product-compliance
Lightning Source LLC
Chambersburg PA
CBHW032109220426
43664CB00008B/1198